# JESUS

Imprimatur
Joseph P. O'Brien
Vicar General
Archdiocese of New York


approved by
The Protestant Council
of the City of New York

**B. GOZZOLI** (1420-1497). "Angels in Adoration" (detail from the "Journey of the Magi").
Palazzo de Medici — Riccardi, Florence.

# JESUS

## HIS LIFE AS PORTRAYED BY THE OLD MASTERS

Commentary
by Père Florent,
of the Preaching Brothers

Paintings selected
by Pierre Belvès,
Director, *Ateliers des Jeunes*
at the *Musée des Arts Décoratifs*

THE
LION
PRESS

Publishers, New York

GENTILE DA FABRIANO (1370-1427). "Nativity." Uffizzi Gallery, Florence.

Published by The Lion Press, Inc.
21 West 38th Street, New York, New York
Published simultaneously in Canada by George J. McLeod Ltd.
73 Bathurst Street, Toronto 2B, Ontario
Library of Congress Catalog Card Number: 69-17726

Printed in West Germany by Mohndruck Gütersloh
©Gautier-Languereau, 1968-French Edition

*No doubt you know who the Virgin Mary is and who Jesus is. Nevertheless, together, we shall start on a delightful journey of discovery. In this book the most famous artists of the past have portrayed this unique history of the birth, public ministry, and death of our Lord and Savior, Jesus Christ. A history? Yes, indeed! And it is not a fairy tale because Jesus lived, as we do know, on this earth for thirty-three years. He had a family, friends — and enemies. All this is written down in an infinitely precious book called the "Gospel:" — the Book of the Good Tidings. The Gospel is the book in which we learn about God's love for all of us, and we shall read some passages from it together. May these brief samples give you the desire to read the whole Gospel by yourselves some day.*

J. VAN EYCK
(ca. 1370 — ca. 1426).
"Palestinian Landscape"
(detail from the altarpiece of "The Mystical Lamb").
Saint-Bavon Church, Ghent.

GIOTTO (1266-1337).
"The Shepherds"
(detail from "Joachim's Dream").
Scrovegni Chapel, Padua.

Just as many families preserve a genea-logy, this is to say — a list of their ancestors, the history of Jesus has also left behind for us the names of illustrious forefathers: beginning with the first man, Adam. The most important were Abraham, Isaac, Jacob, Jesse, David (the great king) and St. Joseph, the adoptive father of Jesus. Others were Joachim and Anna, the par-ents of the Virgin Mary.

A history, of course, is composed of men, women, and children who live in a particular country. The country in which Jesus lived is called Palestine (today it is Israel). It is a tiny country cut up into three regions: in the north Galilee, where Jesus spent his entire childhood (Nazareth, Cana, the lake of Tiberias are located there); in the center lies Samaria, and in the south, Judea, with Jerusalem as the capital. It is here we find the site of the only true Temple.

10

MASTER OF THE LIFE OF THE VIRGIN (XVth cent).
"The Birth of the Virgin."
Pinakothek, Munich.

*Mary, who was to become the mother of Jesus, was born in Palestine. According to tradition, she was presented at the Temple, as Jesus Himself was to be later on. And, as in all the pious families of the Chosen People — the Hebrews — Mary grew up, praying with her parents, listening to and meditating upon the "sacred book," the Bible, in which are written the promises that God made to men. Above all, it contains the promise of a Savior who will come one day to bring men the friendship of God and to open to them, once more, the path to Heaven which had been closed off by sin.*

MASTER OF THE
LIFE OF THE VIRGIN.
"The Presentation
of Mary to the Temple."
National Gallery, London.

14

*Now one day...But here we come to the Gospel in which the whole life of Jesus is told so beautifully.*

...The angel Gabriel was sent from God to a city of Galilee named Nazareth, to a virgin betrothed to a man, whose name was Joseph, of the house of David; and the virgin's name was Mary. And he came to her and said, "Hail, O favored one, the Lord is with you!" But she was greatly troubled at the saying, and considered in her mind what sort of greeting this might be. And the angel said to her, "Do not be afraid, Mary, for you have found favor with God. And behold, you will conceive in your womb and bear a son, and you shall call his name Jesus."

(Luke, I, 26-31.)

17

*It was after this miraculous announcement that Mary went south, near Jerusalem, to the house of her cousin Elizabeth who was to become the mother of St. John the Baptist:*

In those days Mary arose and went with haste into the hill country, to a city of Judah, and she entered the house of Zechariah and greeted Elizabeth. And when Elizabeth heard the greeting of Mary, the babe leaped in her womb; and Elizabeth was filled with the Holy Spirit and she exclaimed with a loud cry, "Blessed are you among women, and blessed is the fruit of your womb! And why is this granted me, that the mother of my Lord should come to me? For behold, when the voice of your greeting came to my ears, the babe in my womb leaped for joy. And blessed is she who believed that there would be a fulfilment of what was spoken to her from the Lord."

(Luke, I, 39-45.)

FRA ANGELICO. "The Visitation." Diocesan Museum, Cortona.

GIOTTO. "Mary's Nuptial Procession." Scrovegni Chapel, Padua.

MASTER OF THE
LIFE OF THE VIRGIN.
"The Marriage
of the Virgin."
Pinakothek, Munich.

*John the Baptist was an amazing man! His birth was announced miraculously by the archangel Gabriel to his father, Zecharia. The latter, astonished by this announcement and somewhat sceptical, was punished for his doubt by being struck dumb until the day of the birth of his son, John the Baptist. On that day Zecharia regained his speech and blessed God with a canticle:*

And his father Zecharia was filled with the Holy Spirit, and prophesied, saying: "Blessed be the Lord God of Israel, for he has visited and redeemed his people, and has raised up a horn of salvation for us in the house of his servant David...And you, child, will be called the prophet of the Most High; for you will go before the Lord to prepare his ways, to give knowledge of salvation to his people in the forgiveness of their sins . . . to give light to those who sit in the darkness and in the shadow of death, to guide our feet into the way of peace." And the child grew and became strong in spirit, and he was in the wilderness till the day of his manifestation to Israel."        (Luke, I, 67-69; 76-77; 79-80.)

*After coming to man's estate, this is precisely what John the Baptist did:*

In those days came John the Baptist, preaching in the wilderness of Judea, "Repent for the kingdom of heaven is at hand."                (Matthew, III, 1-2.)

*Indeed, many people came to see this preacher who lived in the desert, on the bank of the River Jordan. It was here that he preached repentance, calling upon people to be sorry for their sins and to change their lives — to be converted. It was here that he baptized them. Jesus Himself came here in order to let Himself be baptized by His "precursor." This is what Jesus said one day about John the Baptist:*

. . . Jesus began to speak to the crowds concerning John: "What did you go out into the wilderness to behold? A reed shaken by the wind? Why then did you go out? To see a man clothed in soft raiment? Behold, those who wear soft raiment are in kings' houses. Why then did you go out? To see a prophet? Yes, I tell you, and more than a prophet. This is he of whom it is written, 'Behold, I send my messenger before thy face, who shall prepare thy way before thee.' Truly, I say to you, among those born of women there has risen no one greater than John the Baptist; yet he who is least in the kingdom of heaven is greater than he."

(Matthew, XI, 7-11.)

*Such is the person whose feast is celebrated each year on June 24. He has been the favorite subject of many painters and sculptors. And, if some day, you visit the*

PINTURICCHIO (1454-1513). "The Birth of St. John the Baptist." The Cathedral, Siena.

Cathedral of Chartres in France, on the cathedral's north portal you will find one of the most beautiful statues ever created: a statue of John the Baptist holding a lamb in his arm. This is how he referred to Jesus when he pointed Him out to the crowds: "Behold the Lamb of God, who will take away the sin of the world."

PIETER BRUEGEL (1530-1569).
"The Census at Bethlehem."
Royal Museum of Fine Arts,
Brussels.

B. GOZZOLI. "Angels in Adoration" (detail from the "Journey of the Magi").
Palazzo de Medici — Riccardi, Florence.

*Let us retrace our steps, because in the sequence of paintings that we have presented up to now, Jesus has not yet been born. Where are we at this point? ... Mary has had her visitation from the archangel Gabriel in which he announced that she would become the mother of Jesus, the Savior. After that Mary went to help her cousin Elizabeth who was about to give birth to John the Baptist.*

*Now — at that time the world was under the sway of the Roman Empire, especially the Mediterranean basin of which Palestine is a part. It was precisely at the moment that Jesus was about to be born that the Roman emperor wanted to know how many subjects he had under his rule. So he ordered that a census be taken:*

In those days a decree went out from Caesar Augustus that all the world should be enrolled. This was the first enrollment, when Quirinius was governor of Syria. And all went to be enrolled, each to his own city. And Joseph also went up from Galilee, from the city of Nazareth, to Judea, to the city of David, which is called Bethlehem, because he was of the house and lineage of David, to be enrolled with Mary, his betrothed, who was with child.

(Luke, II, 1-5.)

*At long last everything was ready on earth to receive the promised Savior. So, thanks to this census, we know exactly when Jesus was born, and His birth fixes the day among the great events that took place in the world at this time. Now, look at these angels. They see God, they know how much God loves us, and they adore Him. The angels! Alas, you don't see them any more. Yet they do exist, but as pure spirits — without a body. The painters imagined these angels with beautiful faces and sumptuous raiments, because they felt it was necessary to "present" them in an aura of splendor and magnificence. And today, they are here, invisible, near you. And one day we shall be with them in Heaven, and we too shall behold the face of God.*

And while they were there, the time came for her to be delivered. And she gave birth to her first-born son and wrapped him in swaddling cloths, and laid him in a manger, because there was no place for them in the inn.

(Luke, II, 6-7.)

GIUSTO DI GIOVANNI DE' MENABUOI (d. 1393)
"The Nativity." Baptistry, Padua.

HUGO VAN DER GOES ( ca. 1440-1482 ). "The Shepherds."
(detail from the Portinari Triptych ). Uffizi Gallery, Florence.

And in that region there were shepherds out in the field, keeping watch over their flock by night. And an angel of the Lord appeared to them, and the glory of the Lord shone around them, and they were filled with fear. And the angel said to them, "Be not afraid; for behold, I bring you good news of a great joy which will come to all the people; for to you is born this day, in the city of David, a Savior who is Christ the Lord. And this will be a sign for you: you will find a babe wrapped in swaddling cloths and lying in a manger." And suddenly there was with the angel a multitude of the heavenly host praising God and saying, "Glory to God in the highest, and on earth peace among men with whom he is pleased!"

When the angels went away from them into heaven, the shepherds said to one another, "Let us go over to Bethlehem and see this thing that has happened, which the Lord has made known to us." And they went with haste, and found Mary and Joseph and the babe lying in a manger. And when they saw it they made known the saying which had been told them concerning this child; and all who heard it wondered at what the shepherds told them. (Luke, II, 8-18.)

GEORGES DE LA TOUR (1593-1652).
"Adoration of the Shepherds." The Louvre, Paris.

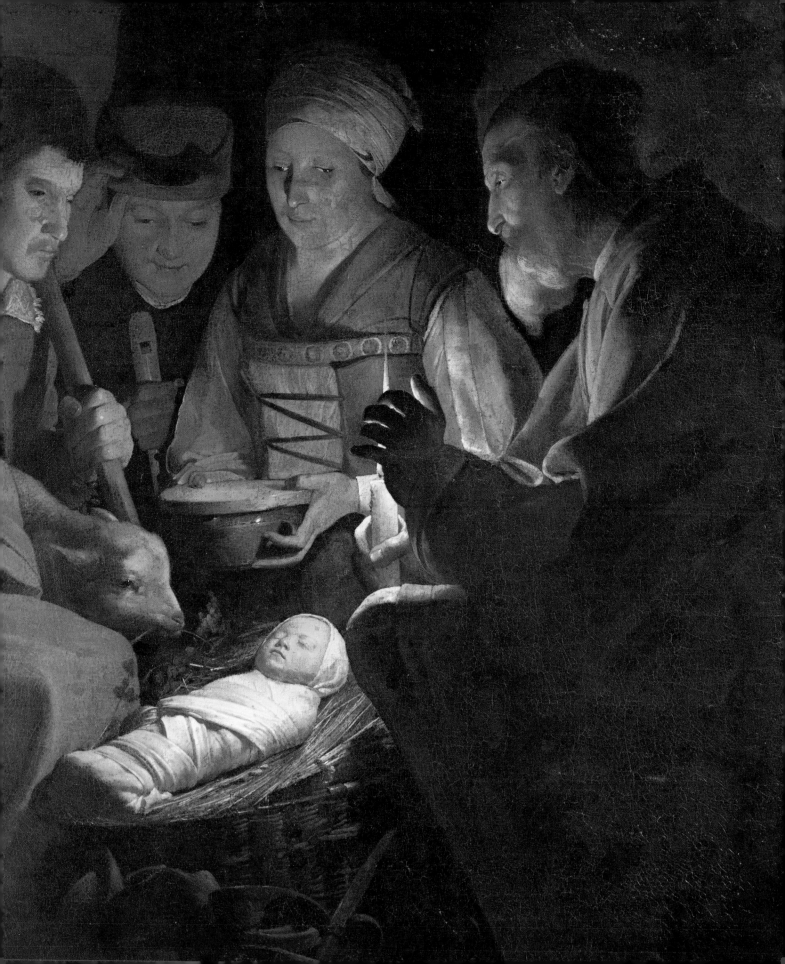

BOTTICELLI (1444-1510).
"Adoration of the Magi."
Uffizi Gallery, Florence.

*After the humble shepherds came those whom we call the "Magi." Today we would call them "astrologers." They were rich and learned men:*

Now when Jesus was born in Bethlehem of Judea in the days of Herod the king, behold, wise men from the East came to Jerusalem, saying, "Where is he who has been born king of the Jews?" For we have seen his star in the East, and have come to worship him.　　　(Matthew, II, 1-2.)

When they had heard the king they went their way; and lo, the star which they had seen in the East went before them, till it came to rest over the place where the child was. When they saw the star, they rejoiced exceedingly with great joy; and going into the house they saw the child with Mary his mother, and they fell down and worshiped him. Then, opening their treasures, they offered him gifts, gold and frankincense and myrrh.

(Matthew, II, 9-11.)

*What is important is that everybody, rich or poor, humble or learned, came to adore this tiny Child who, in His humble manger remains the king of Heaven, come to save and redeem us.*

*32*

"Primitive Virgin."
Church of St. Francis, Rome.

You can see how the artists of all times and of all countries have tried to express their love of the Virgin Mary in paintings and carvings. Their creations are magnificent to behold. Yet when the little shepherdess, Bernadette, was granted the unheard-of privilege of seeing the Virgin Mary appear before her, Bernadette declared that the Queen of Heaven was incomparably more beautiful than the painters had imagined her to be.

34

CIMABUE (ca. 1240-1302).
"Virgin with Child and Angels."
The Louvre, Paris.

BOTTICELLI.
"The Madonna
of the Magnificat."
Uffizi Gallery, Florence.

MASTER OF ST. VERONICA. (XVth cent.). "Madonna with the Ash-Tree Blossom." *Germanisches Nationalmuseum*, Nuremberg.    2. SCHONGAUER (ca. 1445-1491). "Nativity." Pinakothek, Munich.    3. VAN EYCK. "The Virgin at the Fountain." Royal Museum of Fine Arts, Brussels.    4. MASTER OF MOULINS (XVth cent.). "Nativity." *Musée d' Autun*, Autun.    5. VELASQUEZ (1599-1660). Detail from the "Adoration of the Shepherds." The Prado, Madrid.

3    4

*After we have looked at these paintings representing our Heavenly Mother, let us return to the events that surrounded the birth of Jesus. As the Law of Moses prescribed (and as is done by many Christian mothers to this day), Joseph and Mary went to the Temple at Jerusalem "to present" the child, that is to say, to offer Him to God and to thank Him for this birth:*

Now there was a man in Jerusalem, whose name was Simeon, and this man was righteous and devout, looking for the consolation of Israel, and the Holy Spirit was upon him. And it had been revealed to him by the Holy Spirit that he should not see death before he had seen the Lord's Christ. And inspired by the Spirit, he came into the temple; and when the parents brought in the child Jesus, to do for him according to the customs of the law, he took him up in his arms and blessed God and said, "Lord, now lettest thou thy servant depart in peace, according to thy word; for mine eyes have seen thy salvation which thou hast prepared in the presence of all peoples, a light for revelation to the Gentiles, and for glory to thy people of Israel." And his father and his mother marveled at what was said about him. (Luke, II, 25-33.)

40

FRA ANGELICO. "The Presentation of Jesus to the Temple." Diocesan Museum, Cortona.

*But only good and righteous people rejoiced over the birth of Jesus, our Savior. There was also King Herod who, jealous and fearful that this child, whom the Magi had called the "king of the Jews," would remove him from the throne — which he himself had acquired through murder and violence:*

Now when they (the Magi) had departed, behold, an angel of the Lord appeared to Joseph in a dream and said, "Rise, take the child and his mother, and flee to Egypt, and remain there till I tell you; for Herod is about to search for the child to destroy him." And he rose and took the child and his mother by night, and departed to Egypt, and remained there until the death of Herod. This was to fulfill what the Lord had spoken by the prophet, "Out of Egypt have I called my son."

Then Herod, when he saw that he had been tricked by the wise men, was in a furious rage, and he sent and killed all the male children in Bethlehem and in all that region who were two years old or under, according to the time which he had ascertained from the wise men.

(Matthew, II, 13-16.)

42

DUCCIO DI BUONINSEGNA (1260-1319).
"Jesus Among the Teachers."
Cathedral, Siena.

*When the wicked King Herod died, the Holy Family returned from its exile in Egypt. They settled in Nazareth, at that time a tiny hamlet in northern Palestine, in the region called Galilee. Jesus, although the Son of God, wished to live there humbly and without special attention.*

*The ancient Hebrews did not have as many houses of worship as we do today. They had synagogues (halls for meetings and prayers), but in Jerusalem, the capital, there was the grand Temple which every pious Jew was expected to visit at least once a year:*

Now his parents went to Jerusalem every year at the feast of the Passover. And when he was twelve years old, they went up according to custom; and when the feast was ended, as they were returning, the boy Jesus stayed behind in Jerusalem. His parents did not know it, but supposing him to be in the company they went a day's journey, and they sought him among their kinsfolk and acquaintances; and when they did not find him, they returned to Jerusalem, seeking him. After three days they found him in the temple, sitting among the teachers, listening to them and asking them questions; and all who heard him were amazed at his understanding and his answers. (Luke, II, 41-47.)

And he went down with them and came to Nazareth, and was obedient to them; and his mother kept all these things in her heart. And Jesus increased in wisdom and in stature, and in favor with God and man.

(Luke, II, 51-52.)

44

*When He had grown to manhood — He was about thirty — Jesus left Nazareth in Galilee to see John who lived in Judea (in the south) on the banks of the river Jordan, in order to be baptized by him:*

And when he came up out of the water, immediately he saw the heavens opened and the Spirit descending upon him like a dove; and a voice came from heaven, "Thou art my beloved Son; with thee I am well pleased." (Mark, I, 10-11.)

*This is the first public affirmation that Jesus is indeed the Son of God! And now Jesus began preparing for the mission that His Father entrusted to Him. This is why He began a retreat of forty days in the desert where He prayed and fasted.*

And Jesus, full of the Holy Spirit, returned from the Jordan, and was led by the Spirit for forty days in the wilderness, tempted by the devil. And he ate nothing in those days; and when they were ended, he was hungry. The devil said to him, "If you are the Son of God, command this stone to become bread." And Jesus answered him, "It is written, 'Man shall not live by bread alone.'"

And the devil took him up, and showed him all the kingdoms of the world in a moment of time, and said to him, "To you I will give all this authority and their glory; for it has been delivered to me, and I give it to whom I will. If you then will worship me, it shall all be yours." And Jesus answered him, "It is written, 'You shall worship the Lord your God, and him only shall you serve.'"

And he took him to Jerusalem, and set him on the pinnacle of the temple, and said to him, "If you are the Son of God, throw yourself down from here, for it is written, 'He will give his angels charge of you, to guard you,' and, 'On their hands they will bear you up, lest you strike your foot against a stone.'" And Jesus answered him, "It is said, 'you shall not tempt the Lord your God.'" And when the devil had ended every temptation, he departed from him until an opportune time.

(Luke, IV, 1-13.)

*Then Jesus went to the beautiful lake of Tiberias, near Nazareth, a place to which He was often to return because of His great fondness for it. Many events took place here: the miraculous catch of fish; Peter walking upon the water; the storm becalmed. And here Jesus chose His first apostles, from the fishermen of the lake:*

While the people pressed upon him to hear the word of God, he was standing by the lake of Gennesaret. And he saw two boats by the lake; but the fishermen had gone out of them and were washing their nets. Getting into one of the boats, which was Simon's he asked him to put out a little from the land. And he sat down and taught the people from the boat. And when he had ceased speaking, he said to Simon, "Put out into the deep and let down your nets for a catch". . . And when they had done this they enclosed a great shoal of fish . . . When Simon Peter saw it . . . he was astonished, and all that were with him, at the catch of fish which they had taken . . . And so also were James and John, sons of Zebedee, who were partners with Simon. And Jesus said to Simon, "Do not be afraid; henceforth you will be catching men." And when they had brought their boats to land, they left everything and followed him.

(Luke, V, 1-4; 6; 9-11.)

*The lake of Tiberias is completely surrounded by hills; one of them is now called the "Mount of Beatitudes" because it was here that Jesus, before the magnificent panorama of the lake, delivered a sermon containing the essence of the message that He had come to teach to mankind:*

Seeing the crowds, he went up on the mountain, and when he sat down his disciples came to him. And he opened his mouth and taught them, saying:

"Blessed are the poor in spirit, for theirs is the kingdom of heaven.

"Blessed are those who mourn, for they shall be comforted.

"Blessed are the meek, for they shall inherit the earth.

"Blessed are those who hunger and thirst for righteousness, for they shall be satisfied.

"Blessed are the merciful, for they shall obtain mercy.

"Blessed are the pure in heart, for they shall see God.

"Blessed are the peacemakers, for they shall be called the sons of God.

"Blessed are those who are persecuted for righteousness' sake, for theirs is the kingdom of heaven." (Matthew, V, 1-10.)

*48*

*49*

*Jesus began to preach, accompanied by those whom He had chosen — the twelve apostles. But it was necessary for His followers truly to know the identity of Jesus. They understood His sayings, but to make the leap from this understanding to the belief that He was truly the Son of God required many acts of grace. And the first act of grace was that of the Transfiguration:*

And after six days Jesus took with him Peter and James and John, and led them up a high mountain apart by themselves; and he was transfigured before them, and his garments became glistening, intensely white, as no fuller on earth could bleach them. And there appeared to them Elijah with Moses; and they were talking to Jesus. And Peter said to Jesus, "Master, it is well that we are here; let us make three booths, one for you and one for Moses and one for Elijah." For he did not know what to say, for they were exceedingly afraid. And a cloud overshadowed them, and a voice came out of the cloud, "This is my beloved Son; listen to him." And suddenly looking around they no longer saw any one with them but Jesus only.

(Mark, IX, 2-8.)

*Jesus also wished to share the happenings, joys and sufferings of those among whom He lived. One day, along with the Virgin Mary, He was invited to a wedding at Cana, a tiny village of Galilee not far from Nazareth:*

On the third day there was a marriage at Cana in Galilee, and the mother of Jesus was there; Jesus also was invited to the marriage, with his disciples. When the wine failed, the mother of Jesus said to him, "They have no wine." And Jesus said to her, "O woman, what have you to do with me? My hour has not yet come." His mother said to the servants, "Do whatever he tells you." Now six stone jars were standing there, for the Jewish rites of purification, each holding twenty or thirty gallons. Jesus said to them, "Fill the jars with water." And they filled them up to the brim. He said to them, "Now draw some out, and take it to the steward of the feast." So they took it. When the steward of the feast tasted the water now become wine, and did not know where it came from (though the servants who had drawn the water knew), the steward of the feast called the bridegroom and said to him, "Every man serves the good wine first; and when men have drunk freely, then the poor wine; but you have kept the good wine until now." (John, II, 1-10.)

GIOVANNI BELLINI (1400-1470). "The Transfiguration." Correr Museum, Venice.
Following page: GIUSTO DI GIOVANNI DE' MENABUOI "The Wedding at Cana." Baptistry, Padua.

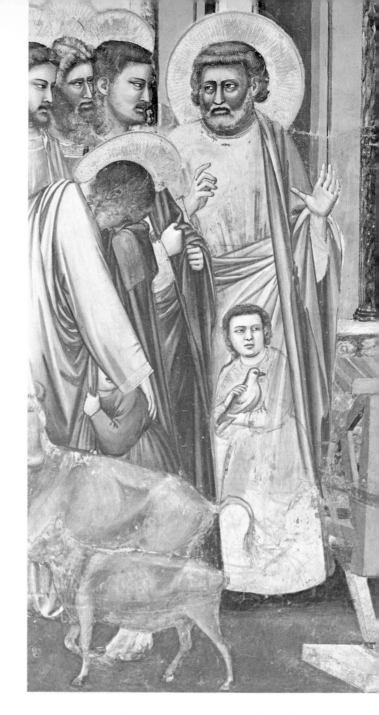

*Jesus roamed through the whole country, preaching wherever He went. He came to Jerusalem and entered the Temple. Here, merchants, and some dishonest peddlers were taking advantage of the piety of the pilgrims who had come to present their offerings, in accordance with the prescriptions of the Law, by cheating them while exchanging their money. At that time there were no banks as we have now:*

And they came to Jerusalem. And he entered the temple and began to drive out those who sold and those who bought in the temple, and he overturned the tables of the money-changers and the seats of those who sold pigeons; and he would not allow any one to carry anything through the temple.        (Mark, XI, 15-16.)

*We have already seen Jesus as an invited guest at a wedding feast and learned about the first miracle that He wrought there. Now, we see Him in the house of a rich Pharisee. Jesus does not work a miracle here, but He takes advantage of an unexpected event to teach His host a lesson, and thereby reminds all of us that we must never sit in judgment on others. God alone, who knows the secret of our thoughts and hearts, will judge the true love with which we have enriched our lives.*

One of the Pharisees asked him to eat with him, and he went into the Pharisee's house, and sat at table. And behold, a

woman of the city, who was a sinner, when she learned that he was sitting at table in the Pharisee's house, brought an alabaster flask of ointment, and standing behind him at his feet, weeping, she began to wet his feet with her tears, and wiped them with the hair of her head and kissed his feet, and anointed them with the ointment.

Now when the Pharisee who had invited him saw it, he said to himself, "If this man were a prophet, he would have known who and what sort of woman this is who is touching him, for she is a sinner."

GIOVANNI DA MILANO. (ca. 1370).
"Repentant Magdalene."
(Detail from the "Repast at the House of Simon").
Church of Santa Croce, Florence.

And Jesus answering said to him, "Simon, I have something to say to you." And he answered, "What is it, Teacher?" "A certain creditor had two debtors; one owed five hundred denarii, and the other fifty. When they could not pay, he forgave them both. Now which of them will love him more?" Simon answered, "The one, I suppose, to whom he forgave more." And he said to him, "You have judged rightly." Then turning toward the woman he said to Simon, "Do you see this woman? I entered your house, you gave me no water for my feet, but she has wet my feet with her tears and wiped them with her hair. You gave me no kiss, but from the time I came in she has not ceased to kiss my feet. You did not anoint my head with oil, but she has anointed my feet with ointment. Therefore I tell you, her sins, which are many, are forgiven, for she loved much; but he who is forgiven little, loves little." And he said to her, "Your sins are forgiven." Then those who were at the table with him began to say among themselves, "Who is this, who even forgives sins?" And he said to the woman, "Your faith has saved you; go in peace."               (Luke, VII, 36-50.)

57

*Let us return to the lake: Jesus loved to dwell on its shores so He could teach His apostles and give them new tangible proof of His Divinity.*

And when evening came, the boat was out on the sea, and he was alone on the land. And he saw that they were distressed in rowing, for the wind was against them. And about the fourth watch of the night he came to them, walking on the sea. He meant to pass by them, but when they saw him walking on the sea they thought it was a ghost, and cried

ANDREA ORCAGNA (ca. 1308-1369). "Jesus Walking on the Waves."
Altarpiece in the Church of Santa Maria Novella, Florence.

out; for they all saw him, and were terri-
fied. But immediately he spoke to them
and said, "Take heart, it is I; have no
fear." And he got into the boat with them
and the wind ceased. And they were
utterly astounded.

(Mark, VI, 47-51.)

*What is the lesson that we must draw
from this miracle wrought by Jesus, walking on the water? St. Matthew gives us
the answer:*

And those in the boat worshiped him,
saying, "Truly you are the Son of God."

(Matthew, XIV, 33.)

*59*

*You have followed Jesus through several stages of His life, especially in connection with what is called His "public ministry": the last three years that He dwelt among us. During this time He taught us the words of God and manifested His power and goodness to us by working miracles. But He has an even greater mission to accomplish: to atone for the sins of mankind, and to make children of God of all those who want to follow Him toward Heaven — the true House of the Father.*

*Thus we arrive at the threshold of the last days of Jesus on earth: He is approaching His Passion, but before that He works a final, striking miracle:*

Now a certain man was ill, Lazarus of Bethany, the village of Mary and her sister Martha. It was Mary who annointed the Lord with ointment and wiped his feet with her hair, whose brother Lazarus was ill. So the two sisters sent to him, saying, "Lord, he whom you love is ill." But when Jesus heard it he said, "This illness is not unto death; it is for the glory of God, so that the Son of God may be glorified by means of it.". . . Then Jesus told them plainly, "Lazarus is dead; and for your sake I am glad that I was not there, so that you may believe. But let us go to him.". . .When Martha heard that Jesus was coming, she went and met him, while Mary sat in the house. Martha said to Jesus, "Lord, if you had been here, my brother would not have died. And even now I know that whatever you ask from God, God will give you.". . .

Then Jesus, deeply moved again, came to the tomb; it was a cave, and a stone lay upon it. Jesus said, "Take away the stone." Martha, the sister of the dead man, said to him, "Lord, by this time there will be an odor, for he has been dead four days." Jesus said to her, "Did I not tell you that if you would believe you would see the glory of God?" So they took away the stone. And Jesus lifted up his eyes and said, "Father, I thank thee that thou hast heard me. I knew that thou hearest me always, but I have said this on account of the people standing by, that they may believe that thou didst send me." When he had said this, he cried out with a loud voice, "Lazarus, come out." The dead man came out, his hands and feet bound with bandages, and his face wrapped with a cloth. Jesus said to them, "Unbind him, and let him go."

Many of the Jews therefore, who had come with Mary and had seen what he did, believed in him.

(John, XI, 1-4; 14-15; 20-22; 38-45.)

*61*

*After the resurrection of Lazarus, we draw nearer to the Holy Week in which Jesus accomplishes that for which God, His Father, had sent Him to earth — our salvation and our redemption:*

The next day a great crowd who had come to the feast heard that Jesus was coming to Jerusalem. So they took branches of palm trees and went out to meet him, crying, "Hosanna! Blessed is he who comes in the name of the Lord, even the King of Israel!" And Jesus found a young ass and sat upon it; as it is written, "Fear not, daughter of Zion; behold your king is coming, sitting on an ass's colt!"

His disciples did not understand this at first; but when Jesus was glorified, then they remembered that this had been written of him and had been done to him. The crowd that had been with him when he called Lazarus out of the tomb and raised him from the dead bore witness. The reason why the crowd went out to meet him was that they heard he had done this sign. The Pharisees then said to one another, "You see that you can do nothing; look, the world has gone after him."

(John, XII, 12-19.)

AMBROGIO LORENZETTI. "The Entry into Jerusalem." Basilica of the Church of St. Francis, Assisi.

*After His hours of triumph, Jesus drew nearer to "His hour"— that is to say the hour in which He was to accept His true mission. It would begin on Holy Thursday and come to an end on the morning of Passover. During this time Jesus sought to demonstrate that His kingdom was not on earth, but was in the hearts of men.*

*You probably know about the beginning of His hour: the Supper — the great repast that Jesus shared with His apostles in that enormous room which we now call the Cenacle. And since in those days, people walked bare-foot in sandals, He washed the feet of His disciples:*

Now before the feast of the Passover, when Jesus knew that his hour had come to depart out of this world to the Father, having loved his own who were in the world, he loved them to the end. And during supper, when the devil had already put it into the heart of Judas Iscariot, Simon's son, to betray him, Jesus knowing that the Father had given all things into his hands, and that he had come from God and was going to God, rose from supper, laid aside his garments, and girded himself with a towel. Then he poured water into a basin, and began to wash the disciples' feet, and to wipe them with the towel with which he was girded.

When he had washed their feet, and

taken his garments, and resumed his place, he said to them, "Do you know what I have done to you? You call me Teacher and Lord; and you are right, for so I am. If I then, your Lord and Teacher, have washed your feet, you also ought to wash one another's feet. For I have given you an example, that you also should do as I have done to you."

(John, XIII, 1-5, 12-15.)

*It was during the Last Supper, that Jesus instituted the Eucharist. As Holy Communion, His sacrifice continues and is repeated at church services throughout the world.*

And when the hour came, he sat at the

table, and the apostles with him. And he said to them, "I have earnestly desired to eat this passover with you before I suffer; for I tell you I shall not eat it until it is fulfilled in the kingdom of God." And he took a cup, and when he had given thanks he said, "Take this, and divide it among

ANDREA DEL CASTAGNO (1423-1457). "The Last Supper." Church of Sant' Appollonia, Florence.

yourselves; for I tell you that from now on I shall not drink of the fruit of the vine until the kingdom of God comes." And he took bread, and when he had given thanks he broke it and gave it to them, saying, "This is my body which is given for you. Do this in remembrance of me."

And likewise the cup after supper, saying, "This cup which is poured out for you is the new covenant in my blood."

(Luke, XXII, 14-20.)

*And now, let us follow the sorrowful events which lead Jesus from the Last*

67

*Supper, where He instituted the Eucharist, to His death. With the help of these paintings, let us engrave on our hearts these moments in which Jesus loved us so deeply that He gave His life for us:*

And they went to a place which was called Gethsemane; and he said to his disciples, "Sit here, while I pray." And he took with him Peter and James and John, and began to be greatly distressed and troubled. And he said to them, "My soul is very sorrowful even to death; remain here and watch." And going a little farther, he fell on the ground and prayed that, if it were possible, the hour might pass from him. And he said, "Abba, Father, all things are possible to thee; remove this cup from me; yet not what I will, but what thou wilt." And he came and found them sleeping, and he said to Peter, "Simon are you asleep? Could you not watch one hour? Watch and pray that you may not enter into temptation; the spirit indeed is willing, but the flesh is weak." And again he went away and prayed, saying the same words. And again he came and found them sleeping, for their eyes were very heavy; and they did not know what to answer him. And he came the third time, and said to them,

"Are you still sleeping and taking your rest? It is enough; the hour has come; the Son of Man is betrayed into the hands of sinners. Rise, let us be going; see, my betrayer, is at hand." (Mark, XIV, 32-42.)

*You know that it was one of the apostles chosen by Jesus who, out of jealousy and greed, betrayed his Teacher to the enemy. But we must not judge. We must only pray because we all are exposed and susceptible to sin. This is what the Gospel says:*

Then one of the twelve, who was called Judas Iscariot, went to the chief priests and said, "What will you give me if I deliver him to you?" And they paid him thirty pieces of silver. And from that moment he sought an opportunity to betray him.           (Matthew, XXVI, 14-16.)

*But when he guided those who were to arrest Jesus, he repented his betrayal.*

When Judas, his betrayer, saw that he was condemned, he repented and brought back the thirty pieces of silver to the chief priests and the elders, saying, "I have sinned in betraying innocent blood." They

ANDREA MANTEGNA (1431-1506). "Christ in the Garden of Olives."
Museum of Fine Arts, Tours.

said, "What is that to us? See to it yourself." And throwing down the pieces of silver in the temple, he departed; and he went to hang himself.

(Matthew, XXVII, 3-5.)

*What a sad end for the Apostle who refused to trust in God's mercy!*

While he was still speaking, there came a crowd, and the man called Judas, one of the twelve, was leading them. He drew near to Jesus to kiss him, but Jesus said to him, "Judas, would you betray the Son of man with a kiss?" And when those who were about him saw what would follow, they said, "Lord, shall we strike with the sword?" And one of them struck the slave of the high priest and cut off his right ear. But Jesus said, "No more of this!" And he touched his ear and healed him. Then Jesus said to the chief priests and captains of the temple and elders, who had come out against him. "Have you come out as against a robber, with swords and clubs? When I was with you day after day in the temple, you did not lay hands on me. But this is your hour, and the power of darkness."

(Luke, XXII, 47-53.)

GIOTTO.
"Jesus Before Caiaphas."
Scrovegni Chapel, Padua.

So the band of soldiers and their captain and the officers of the people seized Jesus and bound him. First they led him to Annas; for he was the father-in-law of Caiaphas, who was high priest that year. It was Caiaphas who had given counsel to the Jews that it was expedient that one man should die for the people.

The high priest then questioned Jesus about his disciples and his teaching. Jesus answered him, "I have spoken openly to the world; I have always taught in synagogues and in the temple, where all Jews come together; I have said nothing secretly. Why do you ask me? Ask those who have heard me, what I said to them; they know what I said." When he had said this, one of the officers standing by struck Jesus with his hand, saying, "Is that how you answer the high priest?" Jesus answered him, "If I have spoken wrongly, bear witness to the wrong; but if I have spoken rightly, why do you strike me?" Annas then sent him bound to Caiaphas the high priest.

(John, XVIII, 12-14; 19-24.)

73

PIERO DELLA FRANCESCA
(ca. 1406-1492). "The Scourging."
Ducal Palace, Urbino.

When day came, the assembly of the elders of the people gathered together, both chief priests and scribes; and they led him away to their council, and they said, "If you are the Christ, tell us." But he said to them, "If I tell you, you will not believe; and if I ask you, you will not answer. But from now on the Son of man shall be seated at the right hand of the power of God." And they all said, "Are you the Son of God, then?" And he said to them, "You say that I am." And they said, "What further testimony do we need? We have heard it ourselves from his own lips." (Luke, XXII, 66-71.)

*Since the people could not condemn anyone to death without the consent of the Romans, who occupied Palestine, they led Jesus to Pontius Pilate, the Roman procurator:*

Then they led Jesus from the house of Caiaphas to the praetorium. It was early. They themselves did not enter the praetorium, so that they might not be defiled,

74

75

but might eat the passover. So Pilate went out to them and said, "What accusations do you bring against this man?" They answered him, "If this man were not an evildoer, we would not have handed him over." Pilate said to them, "Take him yourselves and judge him by your own law." The crowd said to him, "It is not lawful for us to put any man to death."

Pilate entered the praetorium again and called Jesus, and said to him, "Are you the King of the Jews?" Jesus answered, "Do you say this of your own accord, or did others say it to you about me?" Pilate answered, "Am I a Jew? Your own nation and the chief priests have handed you over to me; what have you done?" Jesus answered, "My kingdom is not of this world; if my kingship were of this world, my servants would fight, that I might not be handed over to the Jews; but my kingship is not from the world." Pilate said to him, "So you are a king?" Jesus answered, "You say that I am a king. For this I was born, and for this I have come into the world, to bear witness to the truth. Every one who is of the truth hears my voice."

Pilate said to him, "What is truth?"

After he had said this, he went out to the crowd again, and told them, "I find no crime in him. But you have a custom that I should release one man for you at the Passover; will you have me release for you the King of the Jews?" They cried out again, "Not this man, but Barabbas!" Now Barabbas was a robber. Then Pilate took Jesus and scourged him.

(John, XVIII, 28-31; 33-40; XIX, 1.)

Then the soldiers of the governor took Jesus into the praetorium, and they gathered the whole battalion before him. And they stripped him and put a scarlet robe upon him, and plaiting a crown of thorns they put it on his head, and put a reed in his right hand. And kneeling before him they mocked him, saying, "Hail, King of the Jews!" And they spat upon him, and took the reed and struck him on the head. And when they had mocked him, they stripped him of the robe, and put his own clothes on him, and led him away to crucify him.

(Matthew, XXVII, 27-31.)

76

Following page: Anonymous Portuguese artist (XVth cent.). "Ecce Homo."
Museum of Ancient Art, Lisbon.

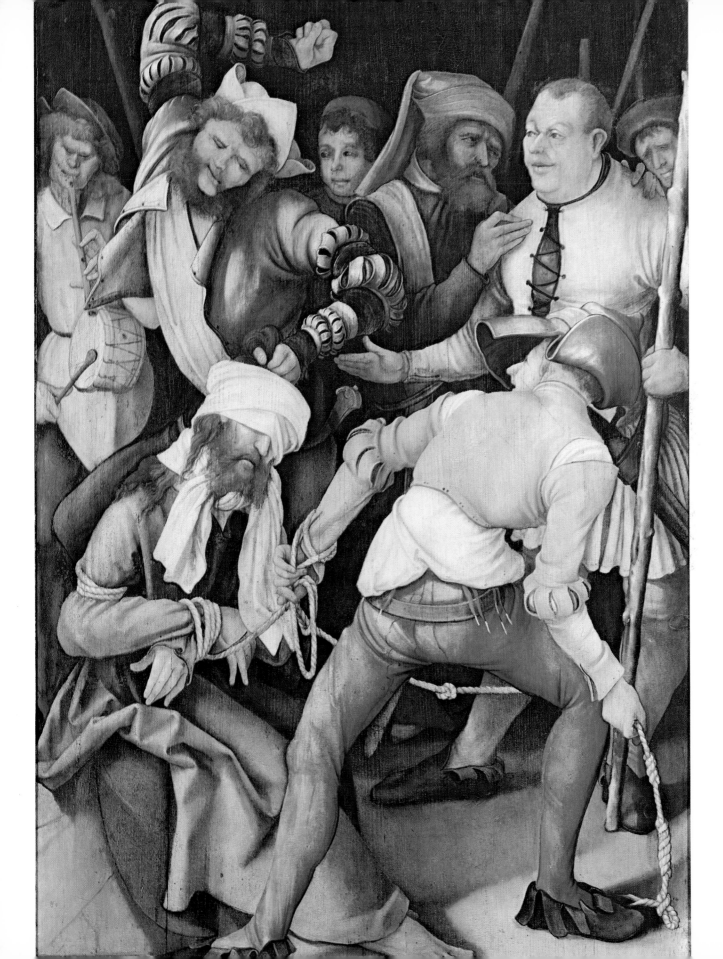

*There is no greater love than to give one's life for that which he loves.*

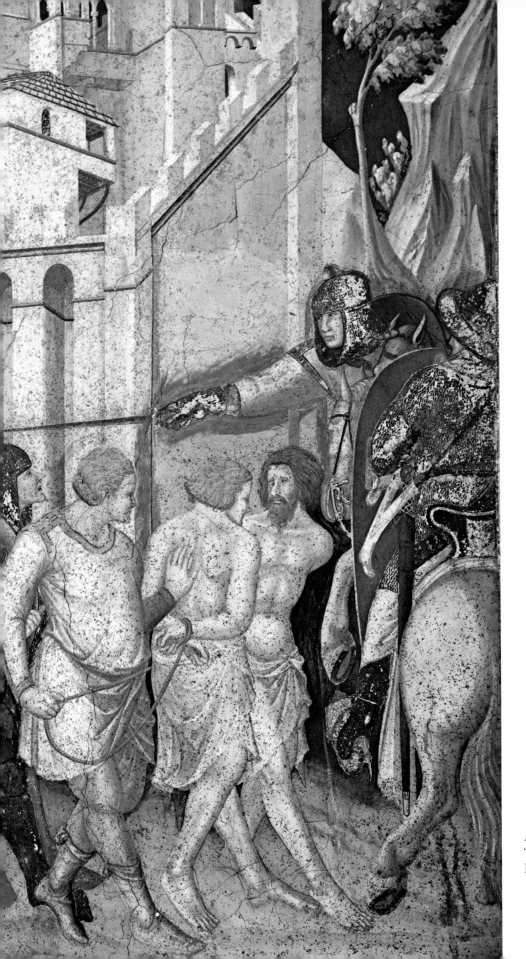

AMBROGIO LORENZETTI.
"The Climb to Calvary."
Basilica of Church of St. Francis, Assisi.

*81*

And as they led him away, they seized one Simon of Cyrene, who was coming in from the country, and laid on him the cross, to carry it behind Jesus. And there followed him a great multitude of the people, and of women who bewailed and lamented him. But Jesus turning to them said, "Daughters of Jerusalem, do not weep for me, but weep for yourselves and for your children. For behold, the days are coming when they will say, 'Blessed are the barren, and the wombs that never bore, and the breasts that never gave suck!' Then they will begin to say to the mountains, 'Fall on us'; and to the hills, 'Cover us.' For if they do this when the wood is green, what will happen when it is dry?"

Two others also, who were criminals, were led away to be put to death with him.          (Luke, XXIII, 26-32.)

So they took Jesus, and he went out bearing his own cross, to the place called the place of a skull, which is called in Hebrew Golgotha. There they crucified him, and with him two others, one on either side, and Jesus between them.

When the soldiers had crucified Jesus they took his garments and made four parts, one for each soldier; also his tunic. But the tunic was without seam, woven from top to bottom; so they said to one another, "Let us not tear it, but cast lots for it to see whose it shall be." This was to fulfil the scripture, "They parted my garments, among them, and for my clothing they cast lots." So the soldiers did this.

(John, XIX, 17-18; 23-24.)

Following page: Wood Sculpture (XIIIth cent.). "The Devout Christ."
Church of Saint John, Perpignan.

It was now about the sixth hour, and there was darkness over the whole land until the ninth hour, while the sun's light failed; and the curtain of the temple was torn in two. Then Jesus, crying with a loud voice, said, "Father, into thy hands I commit my spirit!" And having said this he breathed his last.   (Luke, XXIII, 44-46.)

AMBROGIO LORENZETTI. "The Descent from the Cross." Basilica of the Church of St. Francis, Assisi.

When it was evening, there came a rich man from Arimathea, named Joseph, who was also a disciple of Jesus. He went to Pilate and asked for the body of Jesus. Then Pilate ordered it to be given to him. And Joseph took the body, and wrapped it in a clean linen shroud, and laid it in his own new tomb, which he had hewn in the rock; and he rolled a great stone to the door of the tomb, and departed.

(Matthew, XXVII, 57-60.)

School of Avignon:
"La Pietá of Villeneuve (detail)."
The Louvre, Paris.

At the beginning of the book, the artists showed the mother of Jesus in the joy of Christmas; here we see the Virgin Mary enveloped in sorrow:

"The sorrowful mother, standing before the cross, was in tears at the feet of her dying son.

"Who, without weeping, would be able to look upon the mother of Christ in such torment?

"Grant that my heart burn with such great ardor, so that I may better love Christ my Lord,

And that I may please Him."

GIOVANNI BELLINI. "Pietá." Brera Gallery, Milan.

HAEC FERE QVM GEMITVS TVRGENTIA LVMINA PROMANT
BELLINI POTERAT FLERE IOANNIS OPVS

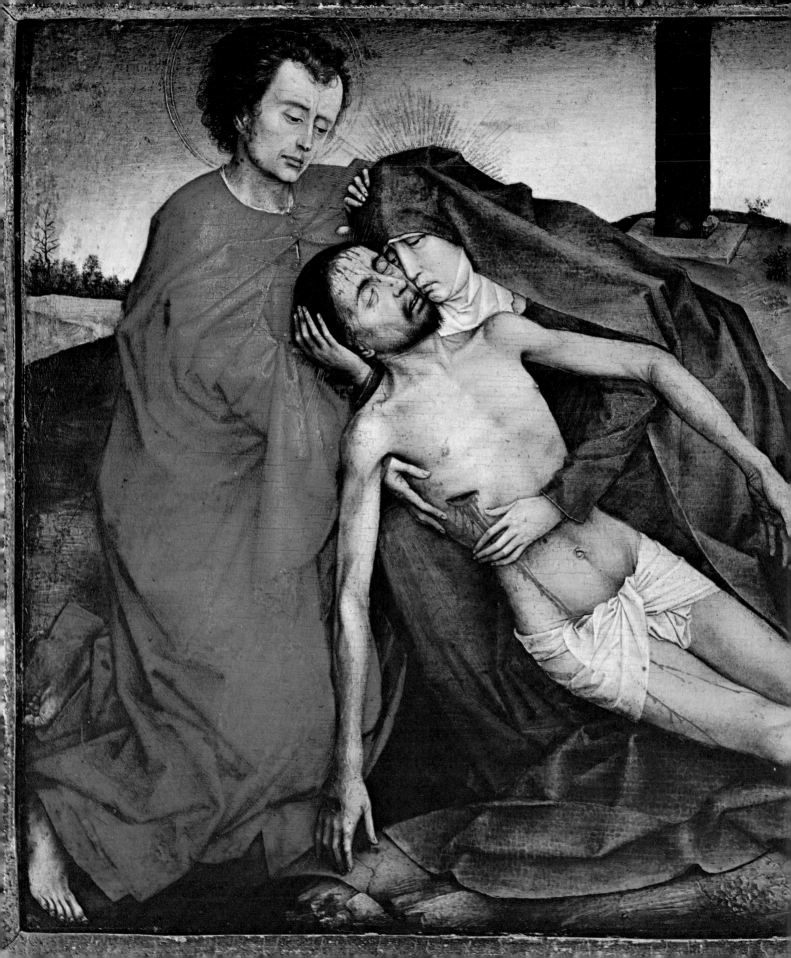

ROGER VAN DER WEYDEN
(ca. 1400-1464).
"Pietá."
Royal Museum of Fine Arts,
Brussels.

*But Jesus had come to conquer sin and death through His redemptive death. And you know how on the morning of the third day — our Easter Sunday — the Holy Women came to the tomb:*

But on the first day of the week, at early dawn, they went to the tomb, taking the spices which they had prepared. And they found the stone rolled away from the tomb, but when they went in they did not find the body. While they were perplexed about this, behold, two men stood by them in dazzling apparel; and as they were frightened and bowed their faces to the ground, the men said to them, "Why do you seek the living among the dead? Remember how he told you, while he was still in Galilee, that the Son of man must be delivered into the hands of sinful men, and be crucified and on the third day rise." And they remembered his words, and returning from the tomb they told all this to the eleven and to all the rest.

(Luke, XXIV, 1-9.)

*Jesus was raised from the dead. But it was necessary that He confirm the certainty of His resurrection to His disciples. And He did this several times during the forty days between Easter and the day of His Ascension to Heaven:*

That very day two of them (apostles) were going to a village named Emmaus, about seven miles from Jerusalem, and talking with each other about all these things that had happened. While they were talking and discussing together, Jesus himself drew near and went with them. But their eyes were kept from recognizing him. And he said to them, "What is this conversation which you are holding with each other as you walk?" And they stood still, looking sad. Then one of them named Cleopas, answered him, "Are you the only visitor to Jerusalem who does not know the things that have happened there in these days?" And he said to them, "What things?" And they said to him, "Concerning Jesus of Nazareth, who was a prophet mighty in deed and word before God and all the people, and how our chief priests and rulers delivered him up to be condemned to death, and crucified him. But we had hoped that he was the one to redeem Israel. Yes, and besides all this, it is now the third day since this happened. Moreover, some women of our company amazed us. They were at the tomb early in the morning and did not find his body; and they came back saying that they had even seen a vision of angels, who said that he was alive. Some of those who were with us went to the

tomb, and found it just as the women had said; but him they did not see."

(Luke, XXIV, 13-24.)

So they drew near to the village to which they were going. He appeared to be going further, but they constrained him, saying, "Stay with us, for it is toward evening and the day is now far spent." So he went in to stay with them. When he was at table with them, he took the bread and blessed, and broke it, and gave it to them. And their eyes were opened and they recognized him; and he vanished out of their sight. They said to each other, "Did not our hearts burn within us while he talked to us on the road, while he opened to us the scriptures?" And they rose that same hour and returned to Jerusalem; and they found the eleven gathered together and those who were with them, who said, "The Lord has risen indeed, and has appeared to Simon!" Then they told what had happened on the road, and how he was known to them in the breaking of the bread.

(Luke, XXIV, 28-35.)

After this Jesus revealed himself again to the disciples by the Sea of Tiberias; and he revealed himself in this way. Simon Peter, Thomas called the Twin, Nathanael of Cana in Galilee, the sons of Zebedee, and two others of his disciples were together. Simon Peter said to them, "I am going fishing." They said to him, "We will go with you." They went out and got into the boat; but that night they caught nothing.

Just as day was breaking, Jesus stood on the beach; yet the disciples did not know that it was Jesus. Jesus said to them, "Children, have you any fish?" They answered him, "No." He said to them, "Cast the net on the right side of the boat, and you will find some." So they cast it, and now they were not able to haul it in, for the quantity of fish. That disciple whom Jesus loved said to Peter, "It is the Lord!" When Simon Peter heard that it was the Lord, he put on his clothes, for he was stripped for work, and sprang into the sea. But the other disciples came in the boat, dragging the net full of fish, for they were not far from the land, but about a hundred yards off.

When they got out on land, they saw a charcoal fire there, with fish lying on it, and bread. Jesus said to them, "Bring some of the fish that you have just caught." So Simon Peter went aboard and hauled the net ashore, full of large fish, a hundred and fifty-three of them; and although there were so many, the net was not torn. Jesus said to them, "Come and have breakfast." Now none of the disciples dared to ask him, "Who are you?" They knew it was the Lord. Jesus came and took the bread and gave it to them, and so with the fish. This was now the third time that Jesus was revealed to the disciples after he was raised from the dead.

(John, XXI, 1-14.)

Then he led them out as far as Bethany, and lifting up his hands he blessed them. While he blessed them, he parted from them. And they returned to Jerusalem with great joy, and were continually in the temple blessing God.

(Luke, XXIV, 50-53.)

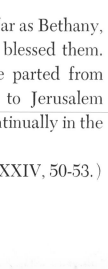

*98*

*My young reader, you have finished reading this book. You have seen what the artists, inspired by the reading of the Gospel of which you yourself have just read many passages, have painted of the life of Jesus. Not everything that Jesus did and said during His earthly sojourn could be related here. What a joy it would be for those who prepared this book, especially with you in mind, if you would now read the whole Gospel from beginning to end! There you will find Jesus in the fullness of His being, with an account of all His words and deeds.*